This book is dedicated to

YOU!

You are special and spectacular.
Show us what you've got!

Your voice might feel as green and slight as a
curled-up sprout. Play. Explore. Argue. Laugh.
Listen. It's growing. Can you hear it? Speak up!

You will make mistakes. That's why we
are so interesting. Every failure is a chance
to learn something new.

Take care of yourself. Need help? Ask! When you
are your best, most bodacious self, the universe
winks and does a little shimmy.

When your dream feels impossible, remember
this story. Be brave. Persist. Work. Grow.
Achieve. Dream bigger.
Shine forward.

—S.W. & G.B.

hmhco.com

The illustrations in this book were created digitally.
The text type was set in Amasis MT Std.
The display type was set in Univers Lt St.

ISBN: 978-1-328-58516-5

Manufactured in China
LEO 10 9 8 7 6 5 4 3 2
4500757343

BEYONCÉ
SHINE YOUR LIGHT

written by Sarah Warren and illustrated by Geneva Bowers

Houghton Mifflin Harcourt

Boston   New York

Beyoncé was quiet.

A push-an-empty-swing kind of quiet.

That's how most of the world saw her, until . . .

one teacher looked closer.
She can sing! Do you know she can sing?

Onstage, Beyoncé became a different person.

Dazzling!

Confident!

Bold!

This was where she belonged.

Beyoncé performed everywhere.
No stage? She made her own.

Beyoncé had a dream.

Someday she'd share her gift with the whole world.

Beyoncé joined a girl group.
They worked hard.
They shared their dreams.
They had each other.

They entered a contest.

They lost.

They learned.

They worked harder.

Beyoncé's family gave it everything they had.
Her mother fashioned them into stars.

Designing

Stitching

Styling

She also paid the bills.

Her father aimed high . . .

Coaching

Planning

Publicizing

It was still Beyoncé's dream,
but other people decided how
to make her dream come true.
Beyoncé paid attention. She learned.

The group performed everywhere.
Wherever they went, they made it
the biggest show on Earth.

Best friends began new adventures.
They cheered each other on.

Before a show,
Beyoncé practiced
until midnight . . .

Until 1 a.m. . . .

Until 2 a.m. . . .

Until 3 a.m.!

She rushed around the world . . .
show after show after show.

An award!

Then another,
then another . . .

Beyoncé knew how to give audiences what
they wanted, and more.
But what did she want?
Beyoncé stopped.
She made time to find the answer.
The world was gigantic. She was just a speck.

Inspired

Lighthearted

Ready

From now on, Beyoncé would be in charge of her dream. She made decisions. Her "no" meant "no." Her "yes" meant everyone gave one hundred percent.

She made mistakes.

She learned.

She grew.

She paid the bills.

She decided what to sing and how to sing it.

When Beyoncé got onstage now, she was herself.
She could also be anything she dreamed up.
So could everyone who sang along.
They could be:

Bountiful

Grateful

Broken

Crazy

Goofy

Jubilant

Regal

Independent

Bright

Angry

Forgiving

Priceless

Healed

The world was her stage.
Where could Beyoncé shine the spotlight?

On new artists

On women

On her hometown in trouble

On the beauty of her people

On the need for justice

Now, Beyoncé finds quiet.
A drown-out-the-noise, get-to-know-herself kind of quiet.
She listens. She keeps dreaming.

QUOTE SOURCE

"*She can sing! Do you know she can sing?*": Darlette Johnson, interview, *The Ellen DeGeneres Show*.

MEDIA

Destiny's Child. Driven Documentary. VH1, 2001.

Beyoncé appearance on *The Late Show with David Letterman*, February 7, 2006.

Beyoncé and Darlette Johnson appearance on *The Ellen DeGeneres Show*, September 5, 2006.

Tina Knowles appearance on *The 2011 Billboard Music Awards*, May 22, 2011.

Beyoncé appearance on *The View*, July 28, 2011.

Life Is But a Dream. Documentary. HBO, 2013.

BIBLIOGRAPHY

Ajayi, Luvvie. "Beyoncé's Lemonade Is Sweet Tea." *Awesomely Luvvie*, April 24, 2016. (www.awesomelyluvvie. com/2016/04/lemonade-beyonce.html)

Bednar, Chuck. *Beyoncé*. Transcending Race: Biographies of Biracial Achievers. Broomall, PA: Mason Crest Publishers, 2010.

Colson, Mary. *Beyoncé: A Life in Music*. Culture in Action. Chicago: Raintree, 2011.

Couric, Katie. *The Best Advice I Ever Got: Lessons from Extraordinary Lives*. New York: Random House, 2011.

Ellison, Jo. "Mrs Carter Uncut." *Vogue*, April 4, 2013. (www.vogue.co.uk/article/ beyonce-interview-may-vogue)

Gottesman, Tamar. "Beyoncé Wants to Change the Conversation." *Elle*, April 4, 2016. (www.elle.com/fashion/a35286/beyonce-elle-cover-photos)

Harris-Perry, Melissa. "A Call and Response with Melissa Harris-Perry: The Pain and the Power of 'Lemonade.'" *Elle*, April 26, 2016. (www.elle.com/culture/music/a35903/lemonade-call-and-response)

Kennon, Michou. *Beyoncé*. Hip-Hop Headliners. New York: Gareth Stevens Publishing, 2011.

McFadden, Syreeta. "Beyoncé's Lemonade is #blackgirlmagic at its Most Potent," *The Guardian*, April 24, 2016. (www.theguardian. com/music/2016/apr/24/beyonce-lemonade-album-video-black-girl-magic-womanhood-america)

Mettler, Katie. "The African, Hindu and Roman Goddesses who Inspired Beyoncé's Stunning Grammy Performance." *Washington Post*, February 13, 2017. (www.washingtonpost. com/news/morning-mix/wp/2017/02/13/these-goddesses-will-help-you-understand-beyonces-grammy-performance/?utm_ term=.4d2be89d4e9a)

Taraborrelli, J. Randy. *Becoming Beyoncé: The Untold Story*. New York: Grand Central Publishing, 2015.

Telusma, Blue. "Beyoncé's 'Lemonade' Is the Love Letter to Black Women We've Been Thirsting For." *The Grio*, April 24, 2016. (thegrio.com/2016/04/24/beyonces-lemonade-is-the-love-letter-to-black-women-weve-been-thirsting-for)

Touré. "Beyoncé Talks Fame, Relationships, Starting a Family, Becoming Sasha Fierce." *Rolling Stone*, March 4, 2004. (www.rollingstone.com/ music/features/beyonce-cover-story-jayz-kids-becoming-sasha-fierce)

Vaughan, Andrew. *Beyoncé*. New York: Sterling Publishing, 2012.

A donation has been made by the author to support a #beygood initiative.

Sarah Warren

is an author and early childhood educator.
She is dedicated to bringing everyday heroes
to life in books that celebrate the diversity
in our schools and communities.
sarahwbooks.com

Geneva Bowers

is a self-taught artist from North Carolina
who loves working with colors and adding
a touch of whimsy and happiness.
genevab.com